Live Cheap and Free!

Strategies to Thrive in Tough Economic Times

Second Edition

Live Cheap and Free!

Strategies to Thrive in Tough Economic Times

Second Edition

Kelly Wilson

DISCLAIMER

This book details the author's personal experiences with and opinions about economical living. The author is not licensed financial consultant.

The author and publisher are providing this book and its contents on an "as is" basis and make no representations or warranties of any kind with respect to this book or its contents. The author and publisher disclaim all such representations and warranties, including for example warranties of merchantability and financial advice for a particular purpose. In addition, the author and publisher do not represent or warrant that the information accessible via this book is accurate, complete or current.

The statements made about products and services have not been evaluated by the U.S. government. Please consult with your own Certified Public Accountant or financial services professional regarding the suggestions and recommendations made in this book.

Except as specifically stated in this book, neither the author or publisher, nor any authors, contributors, or other representatives will be liable for damages arising out of or in connection with the use of this book. This is a comprehensive limitation of liability that applies to all damages of any kind, including (without limitation) compensatory; direct, indirect or consequential damages; loss of data, income or profit; loss of or damage to property and claims of third parties.

You understand that this book is not intended as a substitute for consultation with a licensed financial professional. Before you begin any financial program, or change your lifestyle in any way, you will consult a licensed financial professional to ensure that you are doing what's best for your financial condition.

This book provides content related to topics finances and economic living. As such, use of this book implies your acceptance of this disclaimer.

Table of Contents

Introduction

As a busy wife and mother, I occasionally wonder if the money-saving strategies I've written about and regularly practice are worth my time and energy. Is it worth haunting store aisles for clearance prices on products? What about stockpiling food and gifts to use through the year? Do clipping coupons really save me _that_ much money?

This line of thinking leads me to evaluate what advantages my family experiences as a result of learning to use money wisely. Some of these benefits include:

- No consumer debt
- Purchasing big ticket items with cash (like a King-Sized Mattress set) for one-third of the retail value
- Family vacations and shorter getaways for my husband and me
- Donations of food and other personal and household goods to families and organizations in need

- Lessons in money-management for my children in everyday life

Every time I'm faced with the question of whether or not these strategies make a difference, I decide that doing what I do to save money is well-worth my time and effort.

The first edition of this book was the result of my own personal experiment with becoming a stay-at-home mom, learning to provide what my family needed with just my husband's income. This second edition details how, over the last couple of years, I've continued to learn more about how to save money as some of the rules and conditions have changed. Plus, I've found that the more I practice these strategies, the better I get.

Learning to use money wisely will take planning, patience and discipline. There will be many changes, with the potential to cause anxiety and questions.

I don't know the answers to all the questions, but the strategies outlined in this book have helped save me money and sanity. And I can offer words of hope. It can be done!

Why Do This?

First, I'd like to present my absolute favorite shopping trip of 2009:

Transaction #1 – I picked up a prescription and used a coupon for a $20 gift card with new or transferred prescription purchase. I paid a copay of $20 (that I would have spent anyway and comes out of the copay part of our budget rather than groceries), and received the $20 gift card.

Transaction #2 – I participated in a promotion, spending $25 on certain items (any variety) in order to receive a $10 coupon on my next purchase. This special was in the store's ad, so after careful planning I bought microwave popcorn, ketchup, canned tomatoes, refried beans and peanut butter – all items I could use and my family would eat.

My coupons brought the total to $23.10. I used the $20 gift card and paid $3.10 out of pocket. I also got the $10 coupon for my next purchase.

<u>Transaction #3</u> – There was a special going on with many Betty Crocker items where when you combined items that equaled $10, $4 was deducted. The store's ad made it really easy, in that the similarly priced items were together - such as 4 items for $10, 6 for $10 and 8 for $10, and you could mix and match products.

I bought Nabisco crackers, cereal, tortilla chips, cake mix, frosting, brownie mix, taco shells, pasta, frozen vegetables, and produce, to name some of the products. I bought 10 groups of the spend $10 and deduct $4, so that took off $40. Then I had many, many coupons and used the $10 coupon from Transaction #2.

Final Cost? $50.00, with a savings of $145.94 (the cashier had to get an override...I love it when that happens).

TOTAL Out Of Pocket: $50 + $3.10 = $53.10 with a savings of $164. (I don't count the prescription since it comes from a different part of the budget). OR, $200 worth of groceries for $50.

Every shopping trip isn't this awesome, but it helps me remember why I stick with my strategies.

They save me money. In some cases, a lot of money.

Money that can be freed up to do other things for your family, like a nice vacation or paying off debt. Like planning for your future retirement or your child's education.

More importantly, though, it has taught me the value of good stewardship. I don't waste money anymore. I don't waste food anymore. I've worked too hard to conserve both that I refuse to let them go to waste.

There's also value in sharing. When my children whine about having to give to others, I start the sentence, "Everything we have is for..." and they finish with "sharing." Granted, sometimes their responses sound reluctant. But I'm teaching them a valuable lesson about conserving and giving to others. We are more freed up to donate money or food than we would otherwise be.

Whatever your reasons, make sure you believe them wholeheartedly. This money-saving process is challenging, and requires discipline, attention and perseverance, but it definitely gets easier.

Plus, it's totally worth it!

What Does It Mean To Be Frugal?

Before I started working really hard to save money, I thought that being frugal meant literally pinching pennies, avoiding buying products or paying for services in order to hold on to as much money as possible.

What I found was that I felt deprived – similar to being on a diet – while feverishly denying myself permission to splurge on anything. I found myself buying low-quality products for a little money, and these would soon break or otherwise become unusable. Then I would have to spend additional money buying more low-quality products that wouldn't last.

This kind of money management wasn't working for me, and I didn't like this way of life. I wasn't buying quality products or using services I really wanted at great or even good - prices. I figured that spending money on stuff that wouldn't last was wasting my money and valuable space in my local landfill. I decided to find another way.

I started with using coupons, and I discovered that I could buy products for my family – that we would actually use – for great prices. My pantry began to overflow, and I wasn't spending any *more* money than previous weeks or months.

So I wondered, what could I get by striving to spend even less?

This continues to be my personal challenge, and it is exciting, gratifying, and highly entertaining. I've found my own definition of frugality, which means to spend money wisely on products or services that are really important to me and members of my family.

For example, my husband prefers a specific type of hair product that goes on sale but still tends to be expensive, especially since the company doesn't produce manufacturer coupons. My husband has tried similar products that are cheaper, but he really prefers this particular brand. Even though it's a bit more out of pocket, I buy it for him (on sale, of course) because I know I'm making up the difference in other ways during my shopping excursions.

Another example comes from the reality that some of the food that you can get for a bargain isn't incredibly healthy or nutritious. I like to balance our diet with a variety of fruits, vegetables and lean meat. These add to my grocery bill, but there are also deals on seasonal items, and I consider the added expense worth the money.

Frugal living isn't about self-denial, it's about maintaining balance and shopping with wisdom. As you evaluate your lifestyle and habits when beginning this process of saving money, don't forget to include those items for which you don't mind spending a little more money – by the end of this book, you'll have a variety of ways to get them for great prices!

Getting Started

I decided to start using coupons because I didn't want to pay more than $.50 a box for cereal; this decision started my money-saving process that has brought me to where I am now.

Getting started in this business of saving money can seem overwhelming. My absolute most important piece of advice is to **start small**.

I've included the steps we took in order to get out of debt as well as stick to a budget. It's definitely a process of trial and error, but by going through the experience, you'll be able to figure out what works best for you!

1. Track & Evaluate your spending.

This sounds deceptively simple.

For as long as I can remember, I've had a strange relationship with money. I grew up right at the poverty line. We had food and a place to live, but I was taught to overindulge and then hide from the consequences of overspending, especially through delinquency with credit cards. I didn't know any other way to live than from paycheck to paycheck, avoiding creditors along the way.

As a result, I experience irrational fear when it comes to money. If I had my way, I'd feed my family rice and beans, hoarding away each penny "just in case." If my husband had his way, he'd buy whatever he wanted and not think one minute about saving.

We've had some challenges where money is concerned.

My husband and I have fought through several years of struggling financially. To get out of that rut, we started out simply tracking our spending from day to day, week to week, month to month.

Why? You don't know what kind of money you have until you know where it's going.

Here's a brief example of the budget layout. It's in no way a comprehensive example, but it covers basic expenses:

February 2009

Income	Budgeted	Actual
Jeff's Check		
Kelly's Check		
Gross Income		

Expenses		
Tithe & Compassion		
Life Insurance		
Investment Company		
Mortgage		
Car/Homeowners Ins.		
Gas		
Electricity		
Garbage		
Water/Sewer		
Cable/phone		
Hair Cuts		
Pet Supplies		
Copays		
Auto Rep/Maintenance		
Grocery		
Gas		
Entertainment		
Clothes		
Daycare week 1		
Daycare week 2		
Daycare week 3		
Daycare week 4		
Total Expenses		
Income minus expenses		

I've provided a monthly template if you want to use it (*Appendix A*), and there's also a blank downloadable budget sheet on my website, **www.WilsonWrites.com** *(*under "Free Printable Resources"). Use a budget sheet and spend the next three to six months entering every receipt. **Record every penny**.

The most important part: TELL THE TRUTH.

This is not about guilt. This is not a judgment on where your money goes. It's simply a record of how money passes from one hand to another.

You're going to need these numbers to move on in this process.

2. Start Saving

Even if you dump change into a jar for the next few months, start putting aside some money. This is you, working yourself out of your current job of spending and into this new one of saving. You're going to need some seed money for this venture.

If you can afford to do more, great! Five to ten dollars (or more) a month in a savings account is literally money in the bank. Make sure the amount is realistic for your budget and that you record it on your tracking sheet.

Another way to save money is to spend it by **paying down debt**. _Appendix B_ has a list of websites for more education and information about professionals who can offer assistance, especially if you have considerable consumer debt. If you have a few small balances, concentrate on paying them off one at a time, and at the same time *don't incur any more debt*. Close your accounts, one by one. Cut up the cards and avoid getting new ones.

My husband and I haven't had a credit card for a few years now, and I remember how I felt the first year of our adult lives without one. I was nervous about taking this step. What if there's an emergency?

What we discovered is that if there is an emergency, we have become more resourceful at figuring out different ways to solve the problem. We've also discovered that we can prioritize, and what seems like an emergency can actually wait a week or two until payday. My reliance on credit cards was false security.

Our debt took years to pay off, but be encouraged. With time, persistence and dedication, you can do it!

While you're tracking and saving, use that time to **get organized**.

3. The Cs of Organization

Commitments

If you feel out of control with money, there are probably other areas of your life that could use a makeover.

A few years ago, I felt out of drained, scattered and out of control in my life and I couldn't take it anymore. I decided to make a list of all of the activities to which I had committed. It looked something like this:

- Part-Time Job
- Church Missions Team
- Two Small Children

- Household & Chores
- Church Choir
- Husband
- Girlfriends
- Neighborhood Group
- Church Playgroup
- Preschool Program Volunteer
- Husband's job
- Critique Group

This list didn't necessarily count the activities I *like* to do, like writing, scrapbooking, working out, hiking, biking and going to movies. These, as you can see, didn't even make the list.

Clearly my life needed a change. I was overcommitted and on the verge of a nervous breakdown. It was time to simplify.

I dumped everything – except my husband and kids – and started over. I don't mean to sound flippant, it was actually a very painful process for me over the course of a year. During that time, I gave up my job and all volunteer duties. I focused first on myself, especially since I had contracted pneumonia from simple exhaustion, having endured years of refusing to rest.

Once over that illness, however, I added a little back to my list. Now it looks like this:

- Husband
- Two Small Children
- Freelance Writing for Extra Money
- Writing/Critique Group
- Girlfriends
- Shopping/Couponing
- Other Household Duties
- Fun and stuff I really like to do
- Volunteering at my kids' school and other events

It's a short list. But I feel better. I function better. And money has become a subject that is easier to deal with, especially because I don't feel so out of control.

Calendar

We have a corkboard that takes up the top half of a kitchen wall. Three monthly calendars are pinned up on it, so that we can look about three months ahead. At the beginning of the month, the calendars are adjusted.

There is one hard and fast rule. If an activity needs to be scheduled, it must get written on the calendar. If it's not written on the calendar, it doesn't get acknowledged.

The rest is negotiation – whose activity was written on the calendar first, which activities are job-related (in the case of my husband), which activities happen on a regular basis, and my insanity level from working at home all week and my resulting desperate need to leave the house for an evening.

The calendar is *the key* to a non-chaotic environment. Everything goes on the calendar. It's reviewed daily and weekly.

On a different, very small weekly calendar that hangs on my fridge, I write down each day my plan for dinner and what I'd *like* to accomplish that day. I've provided a template in *Appendix C*.

Monday	Tuesday	Wednesday	Thursday	Friday

Why this extra step? Not everything fits into those small monthly calendar squares, and with changes or conflicts, the calendar can become a mess pretty fast. These daily squares also aid in meal-planning and short notes about commitments, deadlines, appointments and errands.

Plus, I can't write lists. They make me crazy. I can't function with a lengthy list of things that may or may not be important, finished today, or open-ended. The little squares help me define what I *may* be able to accomplish - just today.

Closets

During the next few months of tracking your spending and saving a little, it's time to see **what you can sell**. The easiest way to do that is to go through those closets, including that *really* big closet called the garage.

Go through each room of your house, one at a time. There are three categories by which to judge what you own: Items to Sell, Items to Give Away, and Items Worth Keeping. I even made a list for use in *Appendix D* (also downloadable on **www.WilsonWrites.com** under "Free Printable Resources").

Location (garage, etc.)	Items to Sell	Items to Give Away	Items to Keep

This process can be quite difficult for some people. For me, it's the clothes that don't fit too well anymore, but I'm going to fit into them "again soon." Or it's that really comfortable pair of pants or outdated dress that I "might need again someday." It could be the unattractive vase your Aunt Matilda gave you for Christmas ten years ago, and you keep it to put out in case she visits but she never has visited yet.

Aunt Matilda is never going to visit. Get rid of it!

Garage Sales are great short-term money makers. Plan it for the next weekend of nice weather. Hold one at your house and invite friends to bring their stuff to sell. At least you can have some fun with your friends while sitting in your driveway!

If you don't want to participate in a garage sale, consider selling your more valuable items through local or regional newspaper classifieds. Internet sites like *Craig's List* (www.craigslist.org) are also a great resource for people looking for a good deal, and ads can include pictures of what you're trying to sell. There's also a "Free" section for items you own that you're not interested in selling, and you may be surprised by what people are willing to haul away for free!

An alternative to *Craig's List* is called *Freecycle* (www.freecycle.org), where people give away items to another person who can use them. If you'd rather swap items, *Swap Tree* (www.swaptree.com) makes it very easy – create an account that keeps track of what you want to give away and what you'd like to get from other members, and then swap away!

A much easier alternative is to donate your unwanted items to a thrift store in your community. Keep the tax receipt you receive when you drop off your items. I also make a short list beforehand of what we included in the drop-off; this helps immensely during tax time. Believe me, you won't remember what you got rid of.

4. Analyze Spending

Time to look at the tracking sheets you've spent the last three to six months filling in. It's time to figure out where your money goes!

At the back of this book, there is a sheet provided to help you analyze your tracking sheets (*Appendix E*). Start with observations. Remember, NO GUILT. Make a list of what you see reflected on the tracking sheets. What do you spend money on?

Move on to the Questions. The first one deals with "underspending." Is there an area on the tracking sheet where you are consistently below what you expected? Can this budget item be combined with another budget line? Can it be reduced or even eliminated?

The next question deals with overspending. This is an area where I've been particularly sensitive. Now, after many years struggling with it, I like to say overspending is simply inadequate planning.

For example, last fall I fell ill with pneumonia. I needed several prescriptions and a few extra copays, which cost about $80 over our budget for those areas. It was right around the holidays, so we also had extra car trips to see family and friends, along with Christmas shopping to finish up.

We hadn't planned for these situations, and that resulted in more money gone. But now instead of just blaming myself for overspending, I ask, "What are we not planning for? What plans do we now need to consider where are budget is concerned?" For us, it was setting aside some extra money in our savings account for extra copays and prescriptions, as well as creating a plan for Christmas shopping and travel.

Contemplating cutting expenses can be overwhelming, especially when it looks like there isn't enough money to cover all of the needs reflected in the budget. Which leads to the next question: **What changes can we make**?

I get annoyed by the coffee example – just give up your daily latte and everything will be great! The truth is that most of us, in this economy, probably don't indulge in a daily latte as it is. Don't get me wrong, if you're not making your own coffee and instead buying it every day, it's time to give that up.

What I mean is that the latte example is a bit superficial. I'm talking about lasting change, a shift in how you save, spend and shop. So what can you change? What can you give up?

For me, it started with simply admitting that I can't do whatever I want whenever I want, and as much as I don't like it, I have to talk with my husband about money. We spent a lot of extra time figuring out how we can talk about money in a peaceful way. Then it was much easier to give up those tangible extras, like too many dinners in restaurants and not following a grocery budget.

There are also some other, more drastic, changes to consider. My husband and I started paying off credit cards and then closing all accounts. Then we paid off our cars and vowed not to buy new ones, instead putting our money into regular automobile maintenance. The consequence is that we drive older cars and we have to keep track of oil changes, but it beats a car payment. So are your cars paid off? Can you sell your current car and buy an older, less expensive one?

What about your house? We considered selling our house and moving into something smaller, but considering the current market, it wasn't realistic. Plus we love our neighbors and community. Instead, we researched refinancing our mortgage at a lower rate of interest so we could lower our payment. It provided a little more wiggle room in our tight budget.

Personally, I had to weigh the benefits of cable TV and internet. My husband said that we can give them up at any time; I disagree. I love to watch TV, and I use the internet for my writing business. So for us, we had to compromise with cutting extended cable, which was fine with me. Seventy channels of "basic" cable are already too many.

What can you afford to give up? What about gym memberships with lengthy contracts? Movie rental programs? Restaurant meals? Shopping at big warehouse stores? Cell phone plans? Expensive salon visits?

Based on what you want to change, you'll need to create a monthly budget with a tracking sheet. Keep track of every receipt and whether or not you come out under or over budget each month. Make those hard decisions and stick with them!

The Budget

After analyzing spending and thinking about some goals, it's time to settle on a preliminary budget.

There are several philosophies concerning how to create and maintain a budget. If we haven't tried them all, we've tried several of them. Some programs use cash for everything in an envelope system. Some people use only credit cards with rewards programs to pay their bills and then pay the cards off at the end of the month (we never had the discipline necessary for this plan).

Instead we came up with a compromise. No credit cards at all and a small amount of cash each month for personal use (the occasional cup of coffee or lunch out). We use our debit card for the rest of the budget items, entering receipts into our tracking sheet.

The key to this system actually working is that we meet each week to discuss where we're at concerning the budget and expenditures. This is a good time to get a feel for how much of the grocery budget is left and what bills are coming up. This is valuable information when you see a cute shirt that's on sale for $12.99 while you're out and about; you'll know if you can reasonably afford it.

Granted, the last week of the month is usually pretty tight financially, but it's a process. Try different methods and decide what works for you over time, practice and – yes – mistakes.

5. Evaluate Your Goals

What kind of financial goals do you have?

We had used credit cards all of our married life. We had taken out a second mortgage at an atrocious percentage rate. We had consolidated our debt a couple of times. At one point, we were upside down in our home value-to-debt ratio.

We've made mistakes. And we were tired of fighting about money.

So our most important short-term goal was to live debt-free. Inherently cynical, I wasn't sure how this was going to happen, but it turns out that with hard work and determination, you can do almost anything. Getting and staying out of debt is possible. Start with the smallest debt and pay it off, then the next smallest, then the next.

Our next short-term goal was to have a savings account with three to six months of expenses in it. This is tougher for us, and we're still learning how to keep money *in* the account. But that is our short-term goal, and we continue to work at it.

Don't know anything about investing or saving for retirement? Do some research in your community. Many times, basic investment classes are offered through the parks department or community colleges, either for free or for a nominal fee.

In this economy, I feel a little skeptical when I talk about saving for retirement. If it were up to me and my neurotic feelings about money, I'd hollow out a mattress and keep all of it in there until retirement. But I can't argue with compound interest, and to reach that you have to save long-term. So if you haven't started to save for retirement, start researching. The easiest place to start is the workplace – what kinds of programs do they offer? If not there, gather recommendations from friends and family about where they save money long-term and start making appointments with financial planners.

Are there any other goals you'd like to work toward? Eventually, we'd like to have separate accounts for travel and Christmas shopping as well as saving for our kids' college education.

The irony of this money-saving process for me is that I get such good deals on products and services, but I can *still* overspend.

In the last couple of years, we've made mistakes and had to adjust our budget. The biggest mistake stemmed from our desire to simply not talk about money – my husband and I learned really fast that this simply wasn't wise. We *must* talk about money at least once a week. If we don't, we overspend.

Some of the overspending on my part also has to do with lack of evaluation for where I'm at in this process. After giving so much food away during the last holiday season as well as our desire to save for the purchase of new living room furniture, I decided that I needed more of a challenge when it comes to my grocery budget – my new goal is to **feed my family of four for $65 a week or less**.

I certainly would not have started with this goal, but it seems possible to achieve now - challenging but not discouraging. It's a goal that's appropriate for me at this stage of the money-saving game.

As you travel through this process, take some time each month or so to acknowledge what you're doing well, and what small part of this process needs a little work. And be encouraged - this is a lifestyle you're building, and it won't be finished overnight!

Basic Couponing

Theory of Basic Couponing

If the idea of using coupons raises your blood pressure, I've got a few ways to help you ease into it. It can be an area that's overwhelming, especially if you start subscribing to blogs haphazardly or try to use coupons without basic education.

There's some theory to go along with basic couponing. The first is to **forget brand loyalty** whenever possible. For example, if you are vegetarian or have allergies, there are probably some foods you cannot eat and a coupon will do you no good. But if it's just because you

What coupons should you clip? Whatever you think you'd like to try, especially if you can get it cheap or free! Then store them to use at just the right time.

like the taste of a certain brand of mayonnaise, use a coupon for a different brand instead and branch out. If you don't like that particular brand, it was cheap and you'll know better in the future.

The second theory is **stockpiling**, which is buying a lot of one item when it's available at its lowest price, involving a combination of store sales and coupons. For example, if you can use a combination of coupons that get you a box of cereal for $.60, don't just buy one; **buy as many as you can**! Then use your reorganized pantry to store that cereal to use until another cereal deal comes along (don't worry, it will).

I love big warehouse chain stores, but that's not the kind of stockpiling I mean; prices at these stores are pretty good, but not great. In fact, give up doing the bulk of your shopping at those big chain warehouse stores. This will be a slow – and possibly grief-filled – process, but you can get better deals on the bulk of your grocery and household items in drugstores and standard grocery stores.

Over time, you'll figure out what you can buy at the big warehouse store for a good deal. For example, we have a front-loading washing machine which takes a certain kind of detergent, and the cheapest price I can find is at the big warehouse chain.

When you start **practicing stockpiling**, your shopping trips will become focused and seem too narrow. You'll still need to buy the basics like milk, eggs, bread, and fruits & vegetables, but you'll probably also be buying ten to twenty boxes of popcorn or cereal at once, combining coupons to such a degree that you'll get them for pennies instead of dollars. The nice thing about stockpiling is that you won't need to buy cereal or popcorn for several weeks, and you'll have extras to give away. It seemed odd to me at first to shop this way, but it actually saves me a bunch of money each month.

Don't want to run out of money for groceries? Make a weekly grocery budget as you're starting to stockpile ($40 - $80 a week). Once it's gone for the week, it's gone! This will help balance need and want.

The third basic theory is to **pay attention**. This is accomplished mostly through studying ads, reading blogs and talking with others. It's my understanding that grocery stores work on a twelve-week cycle, and that sales and coupons follow that pattern. You'll learn through practice which items cycle; for example, it seems to me like toothpaste is *always* on sale somewhere, and there is often a coupon to use with the sale and I almost always get it for free. Other items, like cleaning products, are on sale less often and there are fewer coupons, so grab as many as you can when the prices are low and there are coupons to go with the sale. Some manufacturer coupons also come out on a regular basis. There are often diaper coupons, but not many, and

> *Too overwhelming? Log on to The Grocery Game (http://www.thegrocery game.com/) for a system that's already done for you and will cost you very little. Once you're ready to go out on your own, cancel your subscription.*

there are rarely sales on diapers. So when you find a good match, stockpile!

Practice of Basic Couponing

My absolute best words of advice: **Start Small**.

Store ads and coupons come in the Sunday paper. Manufacturer Coupons come in ad inserts from *Smart Source, Red Plum* and *Proctor & Gamble.*

Start purchasing a **Sunday paper** each week. For awhile, I had it delivered to my house, which cost about $12 a month. Plus, our city's newspaper delivers ads to neighborhoods (called "Food Day") each Tuesday at no cost. The Safeway double coupons come from this weekly paper. It would be worth a phone call or email to your city's newspaper to see if they provide a similar service.

> *Sign up for store programs that use membership cards or offer rewards.*

On Tuesday morning, I pour a cup of coffee and grab my "need to get" shopping list, along with more notepaper to take notes about the ads. I match up grocery stores' deals with what I need to get and make notes of any good deals that are to my advantage, going through my supply of manufacturer coupons. I keep these ads in a safe place to review them again on Sunday and finalize my list for the week.

On Sundays, usually the only store ad is from Fred Meyer in my area, so I take note of any great deals. I take all of the ads out of the newspaper and start clipping manufacturer coupons that I like to carry with me. Then, based on my notes and coupons, I plan my shopping trips.

There are four basic stores on my route and are listed in my order of importance: Fred Meyer, Albertson's, and Safeway for grocery items, and Walgreen's and Rite Aid for household and beauty products. They all have store coupons and also accept manufacturer coupons. Each store has its own particular advantages.

Store Analysis

Stores, coupons and even prices vary by region, so I've included an example of how I prioritize the stores in my area that offer the best consistent deals. Analyzing Grocery Stores (Appendix G) can also be used to make notes about stores in your area.

Fred Meyer has quite successfully adapted to the downturn in the economy, so that many of what are considered staple items are at consistently competitive low prices. For example, loaves of bread (even whole wheat) range from $.99 to $1.50 each and milk is around $2 to $2.50 a gallon (less on a coupon).

Fred Meyer has a Rewards program (http://www.fredmeyer.com/MyFredMeyer/Pages/rewards_FAQ.as px) with a card you need to use with each transaction. There are specific Rewards cycles throughout the year (look at the bottom of your receipt for specifics), and each purchase total contributes to

your Rewards amount.

This sheet, downloadable on www.WilsonWrites.com, will help you analyze grocery stores in your area.

Name of Store	Ads with Store Coupons Available?	Accepts Competitors' Coupons?	Has or Accepts Double Coupons?	Rewards Program or Bag Credit?

At the end of the last Rewards cycle, I received $13 worth of vouchers to use like cash at Fred Meyer, along with some awesome in-store coupons not available anywhere else outside of the Rewards program.

In addition, Fred Meyer runs weekly ads that consistently offer great deals on cereal, bread, milk, juice, cheese and household items. These store coupons can be combined with manufacturer coupons for greater savings.

Albertson's has a "Preferred Savings" program that requires the use of a card in order to save. These specials can be combined with store and manufacturer coupons, which can generate some great deals.

The latest – though inconsistent – coupon at Albertson's is the double coupon. These double coupons often come in the Sunday paper in groups of 3, and each coupon doubles a manufacturer coupon up to $1 in value. This is a potential of $3 off the total of your bill. However, my experience is that they do tend to be rigid about coupons that say "do not double," and won't double a coupon over $1 in value.

Safeway has their "Club Card" program, so make sure you sign up and use it during each transaction. They usually have wonderful store coupons

If a store runs out of a product that's on special, request a **raincheck**! *Just make sure you redeem it before manufacturer coupons expire.*

along with coupons you can electronically load onto your Club Card. Safeway also has double coupons in their weekly ads that match up to $.50 of manufacturer coupon. There are four double coupons for a potential total of $2 off your bill.

Safeway also prints "$10 off a $50 total purchase" coupons in weekly or Sunday ads at a rate of about one for every four to six weeks. Make sure you read the fine print on these – sometimes the $50 is before manufacturer coupons but after store coupons are used, or other restrictions apply. Ask store management *before* you start shopping concerning restrictions on these particular coupons if you have any questions.

Walgreen's doesn't have a store savings card nationally, but is currently piloting one in certain markets around the United States. For those areas without the card, Walgreen's has great sales and store coupons, along with their "Register Rewards" program.

Register Rewards are coupons printed at the register – also called catalinas - that you receive for your next shopping trip and can be used like cash. They are based on how much you buy of a product or products on special in a given week; for example, buy two cough medicines at 2 for $6, get $3 in Register Rewards. Say the cough medicines regularly retail for $5.99 each – 2 for $6 is already a great sale. Then you use a manufacturer coupon for $1 off 2 of those cough medicines, paying $5 and getting $3 back in Register Rewards. You've essentially paid $1 per bottle of cough medicine instead of the regular price of $11.98. These are tremendous savings!

Be aware, however, that Register Rewards ring up as **manufacturer coupons**. Walgreen's doesn't allow the use of more manufacturer coupons than purchased items; for example, if you have five items and five **manufacturer coupons** already, then the Register Reward will not be accepted because it is another manufacturer coupon (store coupons don't count toward this final coupon total). The way to deal with this is to provide what's called a "filler" item, which could be something that you need that's relatively inexpensive, or an item that is less than $.50 in order to maximize your savings.

Rite Aid has a variety of different programs in addition to producing ads with store coupons that can be combined with manufacturer coupons. The first is called "Single Check Rebate," and in this program there are items each month that qualify for rebates from Rite Aid. In order to receive the rebate, you must purchase the items and then submit your receipt either online or by mail. You can submit as many receipts as you want during the time period (usually a month long), then request your Single Check Rebate at the end of the month. They send you a check for your rebate amount through the mail that you can use at Rite Aid like cash.

The second program at Rite Aid is more inconsistent, but very easy to participate in. This program is called the "Season of Savings," and in my experience runs quarterly (though not necessarily *every* quarter). During the fall quarter, for example, you simply had to submit receipts online or through the mail (like the Single Check Rebate program), and the rebate rewards depended upon what you spent. For a $20 total purchase, *regardless of the products purchased*, there was a $5 reward – the rewards increased along with how much the receipts totaled for that time period.

The last two programs are relatively new. One is called "Wellness Rewards" and one is called "+UP Savings." The first is a program where extra savings are available if the consumer uses a Wellness card, which is basically a store loyalty card. The second program involves coupons (similar to catalinas) that print out on each receipt, such as "$1 off a $10 healthy and beauty purchase." At this point, these +UP coupons are in addition to any store and manufacturer coupons used in a transaction.

Personally, I think the best part about the Register Rewards and Single Check Rebate programs is that it doesn't matter if you use store or manufacturer coupons together to complete a transaction. A brand of deodorant could be $3.99 regular price, but on sale for $2.50 with a $1 Single Check Rebate. Even with the Single Check Rebate, you can still use the $1 on one manufacturer coupon for that deodorant that you have in your coupon file. This would make the $3.99 deodorant fifty cents ($2.50 - $1 manufacturer coupon - $1 Single Check Rebate = $.50). Because of that there are many items that, when it all shakes out, end up costing next to nothing.

I get questions about how grocery stores like Food 4 Less and Winco compare to shopping other stores with coupons. I used to shop at both of these stores regularly, and friends of mine and I have compared prices at these two stores with ads from other grocery chains. Each time, the ad prices are lower, and if you combine those ad prices with store and manufacturer coupons, the prices are even lower still.

> *What about stores like Costco? Figure out the price per unit to make sure you're getting a good deal on a product in bulk.*

Another issue concerns specific grocery stores that don't operate in my area, such as Top Foods, Randall's, and Wegman's to name a few (http://www.pugfound.com/grocery.html), and you might not shop at the same stores I mentioned above. If this is the case, use the strategies in general – who has double coupons? Which stores take other store coupons? Appendix G can help you figure all of that out.

Coupon Policies

One of my personal frustrations in this money-saving process is the inconsistencies of store coupon policies. When I first started couponing, I didn't understand that it would be a good idea to have copies of these coupon policies to whip out in case I ran into a problem with a cashier or manager during a transaction.

> _Stores like Walmart and Target practice price-matching. Make sure you have the ads with for the items you want stores to price-match!_

Now I have copies of coupon policies safely tucked into my coupon organizer, available at a moment's notice! Here are the website addresses for major chain stores so that you can print your own copies to take with you. You may have to email customer service since many chains do not put their coupon policies on the web, and my experience is that someone will reply with the requested information in a reasonable amount of time.

Store Website For Coupon Policies

Walmart - http://walmartstores.com/7655.aspx

Target - http://www.target.com/b/ref=br_bx_4/192-9168409-2594745?ie=UTF8&node=2223357011

Walgreen's - http://www.walgreens.com/marketing/contactus/default.jsp?foot=contact_us

Albertson's – Go to www.albertsons.com, then "Contact Us" at the bottom of the page

Safeway - http://www.safeway.com/IFL/Grocery/Coupons-Policy

Fred Meyer - http://www.fredmeyer.com/Pages/default.aspx, then "Contact Us" at the bottom of the page

Rite Aid - http://www.dealseekingmom.com/wp-content/uploads/2009/10/Rite-Aid-Official-Corporate-Coupon-Policy.pdf

Once you start carrying these coupon policies around with you, don't be afraid to use them. If there's a problem with a coupon or transaction, be polite and ask for clarification. I like to have checkers or managers go over it with me when there's a problem, requiring them to use the corporate coupon policy to defend their answers.

If you still can't come to a reasonable outcome after trying to work out your particular situation, decline to purchase the product in question. I've had situations where I *know* I'm in the right and the corporate policy has backed me up, and I've had to leave without purchasing anything at all. If this happens to you, consider contacting the corporate office concerning your situation, politely and calmly providing names and details.

I've provided a template for composing a complaint on the following page (this template is also downloadable under the "Free Printable Resources" on www.WilsonWrites.com).

Useful Complaint Template

<Greeting>

My name is *<**Your Name**>* and I frequently shop at *<**store name**>* at *<**store location**>.*

On *<**enter date and time**>,* I had a problem with purchasing a product at your store. *<Explain **the facts** of the problem – emotions are next.>*

As a result of this transaction, I feel *<**supply your own feeling words**>.* I feel this way because *<**state your reasons**>.* I would like a resolution to this problem. *<**This is VERY IMPORTANT – state how you want the problem to be solved to your satisfaction**>.*

You can contact me at *<**contact information here**>.*

Thanks,

*<**Your Name**>*

Whether or not I've liked the response, I've always received one.

Someplace for Your Stash

Once you start shopping for bargains, you'll soon have a healthy stockpile of food and household products. Stockpiling is simply buying products at their lowest price in the 12-week grocery and coupon cycle that will last you until they reach the next rock-bottom prices.

I'm not scientific about figuring out exactly when these rock bottom prices will occur – I have enough experience now that I recognize a great price when I see it, and my stockpile of products makes it necessary for me to not buy much when I _need_ it, since what I need is already there.

Because I'm such a good bargain and coupon shopper, however, I sometimes struggle with where to put my stockpile.

Spend-Save-Split

It seems anti-intuitive to spend more to save more, but this is often the case, especially when using coupons. Prices are often based on quantity and grocery stores use this strategy all the time; products are advertised "2 for $6" in order to make you think that you must buy two products to get the price, and two for $6 seems like a better deal than one for $3.

A common question is that if products are priced ten for $10, are we required to buy a quantity of ten to get this price? The answer – most of the time – is no. However, if there are restrictions on the price, there will be fine print in the ad and displayed with the product. Usually, you can just buy the quantity you want and still receive the sale price.

It's important to remember that *savings is calculated per unit*. A common scenario involves a product – let's say pasta – priced at $1.50 each. Then I find a coupon for this brand of pasta, which states $1 off a purchase of 3 packages, and I also have a double coupon that is worth up to $1.

I could buy three packages for a total of $4.50, minus the $1 manufacturer coupon and the $1 double coupon, for a final total of three packages for $2.50. The *per unit* price is $.83.

This is a great price, and it would be smart to buy more and stockpile. I have multiple $1 manufacturer coupons, and since the coupon states that I save $1 on a purchase of three, I decide to buy six packages for a total of $9.00.

Then take off two $1 manufacturer coupons and two $1 double coupons for a final total of $5. But what if you already stocked up on pasta a few weeks prior, and you don't want or need six boxes?

Split it.

I shop with two other families on a regular basis. As ads come out on Sundays and Tuesdays, I write down the deals I'd like to take advantage of, and then I email the other two families my plans. They indicate whether or not they're interested in these specific deals, so I shop, email the amounts the food cost, and they pay me back when they pick up their groceries from me. We all save *more* money than by shopping alone because we buy in larger quantities and then split the cost.

Utilizing Closet Space

One of my challenges over the last few years has been where to put my stockpile of food and household goods. Earlier in this book I talked about "The 3 C's to Organization," and specifically about cleaning out those closets. If you haven't yet done that, now is a good time – you'll need the space for your stockpile, and you can make some extra cash by selling stuff you don't use or need.

When those closets and cabinets are cleaned out, consider the following tips to organizing your stash of cheap and free products.

Chances are you have more space than you realize. There are closets in every bedroom, usually a pantry and linen closet in the hallway, and maybe an additional storage or coat closet somewhere in the house. If you have a basement, then there's the benefit of that additional space.

I like to keep my stash organized by room. Non-perishables go in the pantry, cleaning products go underneath the sink, bathroom products are stored in the bathrooms, and toilet paper and other household goods go in the linen closet. Downstairs is what we call "The Gift Closet" where potential birthday and Christmas gifts go into non-transparent totes, as well as health and beauty items set aside to be given away families and organizations in need.

This system may not work for you, and it might be a good idea to try out a few different ways of storing your cheap and free stuff. I've read of families who keep everything in a giant pantry, organized by product type, and friends of mine use shelves they've put up in their basement specifically for this purpose. Regardless, I encourage you to take some time to set up a system of organization to help take advantage of those deals you worked so hard to get.

Organizing the Food Closet

Not too long after I started using coupons, I had more food than I knew what to do with. This is fine, unless your Food Closet (or pantry) gets out of control!

It happened gradually, and pretty soon I couldn't find the pasta I *knew* I had purchased for $.25, and it drove me crazy! We cleaned everything out, and my husband came up with a system to keep the Food Closet orderly.

First, we organized by type of food. Canned tomatoes, soup, spaghetti sauce, pasta and other side dishes were stored together. In a different area, there were granola bars, breakfast bars, cereal, and crackers. Then sauces, pickles, dressing, and other bottled goods were put together. Put the food together in ways that make sense to you, and items will be easier to find.

Then we figured out what seems quite obvious – the bigger products can still be seen from the back of the closet. So we organized the products by size – short in the front, tall in the back, and similar items stacked two cans high.

The organization of the Food Closet depends on the products we have at any given time, which fluctuates a little due to what we've used versus what's a great deal that I recently purchased to stockpile. As you work with your stockpile, don't forget to constantly push forward – as you buy and shelve, put the newest products at the back of the closet, bringing the older ones forward so they can be used!

Make Room For Extras

I haven't always loved Christmas, but one of the reasons I do now is that by the time December rolls around, I usually have bags full of cheap and free items I've collected through the year to give to organizations that feed families in my community. I especially like to store bath items and household goods – people have a need for them and these products tend to be more expensive, and they aren't among the items frequently donated.

While I'm stockpiling for my own family, I use the Gift Closet downstairs to not only store possible birthday and Christmas gifts, but also to store totes or bags of items to give away. Each time I shop, I get in the habit of finding at least one cheap or free item to set aside in this closet, and pretty soon there's a separate stockpile. And I don't have to wait until December – there are many opportunities throughout the year to donate needed items to charitable organizations.

As you begin to stockpile your cheap and free finds, set up an organizational system that works for you – it will help save you money throughout the year!

But What About Expiration Dates?

If you've ever had food poisoning, then you are probably aware of how important it is to follow food-safety rules.

Stockpiling is important when it comes to shopping to save money, but all of these "use by" and "best by" and "expiration dates" can be confusing. Here's a breakdown of what it all means!

- **Use-By, Best if Used By, Best By, Best Before** – These dates are usually found on non-perishable food items like ketchup or peanut butter. This is not a date regarding safety, but it does tell us when a product might change in flavor, texture or color. As long as the item has been and continues to be stored properly, it should be fine. However, trust your nose when it comes to eating them – if it smells funny, skip it!

- **Sell By** – These dates are usually found on dairy and meat products, and help grocery stores keep track of and rotate their stock. Food is usually good for awhile after the "Sell By" date.

- **Expires On** – These specific labels and dates are found on foods regulated by the federal government, like baby formula. It's important to not consume food after the "Expires On" dates.

Other letters and numbers that often appear jumbled are packing codes. These are generally for store use and help with inventory and recalls.

If food goes bad before you get the opportunity to use it, it will be doubly disappointing since you worked so hard to save money on it. There are ways to help lengthen shelf life through storage options:

- Always rotate your stock, using the oldest products first.

- When you buy items in bulk, vacuum seal them for longer shelf-life.

- Place foods in a cool, dry, dark location.

- Use air-tight containers for opened products, like flour, sugar, cereals and crackers.

No matter what the date says, **Trust Your Nose** if there's ever a question about a food product! I've had cheese smell bad long before the expiration date due to poor packaging, and when I contacted the company, they sent me coupons to replace it. Always practice safety while making the most of the foods in your stockpile!

Advanced Couponing

When I started couponing seriously and consistently, I discovered that the money-saving world has its own rules, vocabulary and abbreviations. It became a little challenging to keep track of all of the terms, so I've provided the following glossary to help.

This glossary is available as a free printable at www.WilsonWrites.com.

Term	Definition
Catalina	A coupon that prints out from the cash register after a transaction has been completed.
Double Coupon	Coupon issued by a store that matches the value of a coupon up to a certain amount. For example, a double coupon from Safeway matches up to $.50 of the value of a coupon.
"Food Day"	Oregon's Tuesday ads delivered to homes free of charge.

Internet Printable	A coupon printed at home from an internet source.
MC	Manufacturer Coupon, stated by the expiration date at the top of the coupon. Issued from the company that makes the product.
OOP	Out of Pocket – how much money actually spent on a transaction after coupons, rebates and gift cards.
OYNO	On Your Next Order (Purchase)
Raincheck	A form from a store when a product is out of stock. Allows customer to buy the product when it comes in at the sale or coupon price.
Rebate	Money issued to the consumer after conditions of a rebate have been met, usually by submission of a form, receipt and UPC symbol.

RR	Register Rewards are catalinas issued by Walgreen's after purchase of specific products. They are like cash for use at Walgreen's.
SC	Store Coupon, issued by a store usually through a Sunday or Tuesday ad and only accepted at that store.
Scenario	A plan to buy certain items using discounts, store and manufacturer coupons, and rebates in order to get the lowest price.
SCR	Single Check Rebate – a program operated by Rite Aid. Submit receipts each month for specified items (online or through the mail) and request the rebate at the end of the period. *Rebate can only be processed once each period.*
Stack	The strategy of combining store specials, store coupons and manufacturer coupons for maximum savings on products.
Transaction	Where money is exchanged for products.

UPC	Symbol found on products, usually in barcode form.
YMMV	An abbreviation for "Your Mileage May Vary," which refers to the possibility that the possible deal might not work out the same for one person as another.

The Trifecta

The magic of couponing happens when three elements come together – the store sale, the store coupon (this can include double coupons), and the manufacturer coupon. Over and over again, I've found that combining these three elements saves loads of money.

It's time to do some more research and take more notes. Appendix G has a spreadsheet you can use to record what you like about different stores that take coupons. Don't forget to scout out drug stores as well as grocery stores. If the drug stores have their own store coupons, you can **stack** those with manufacturer coupons and save more.

Store coupons are put out by the store to promote the sale of certain items. In most cases, they are only accepted by the store that generated them.

How do you know a coupon is for real? Check out the Coupon Information Corporation (www.cents-off.com). There, you can access a list of counterfeit coupons.

Manufacturer coupons, however, are generally from the larger corporations that produce brands, like Kraft and Betty Crocker. The important thing to remember about manufacturer coupons is that the store gets reimbursed for their value. These coupons can be found mostly in ads in the Sunday paper or by signing up with the corporation (we'll get to that later).

Manufacturer coupons can also be found online, though availability is limited. If I have a store coupon for Kraft salad dressing and I want a manufacturer coupon, I look in my accordion file first. If I don't find it, I can do a search online, but that doesn't mean I'll find one ready to print. If a coupon becomes available to print, then print it right away! Companies limit the amount of coupons they will allow consumers to print, and when they're gone, they're gone.

Regardless of what you're looking for, when there's a deal that involves the Trifecta, I have a hard time turning it down. There's no magic like combining store sales, store coupons and manufacturer coupons for the lowest prices on products.

Organizing Coupons

At this point, I don't go anywhere without my coupons, which is partly why they're in smaller accordion files. I also keep the accordion files in my car if I don't feel like lugging them around in my purse. I use two of them, one for drug stores and one for grocery stores. I'm thinking of purchasing a third just for rebate forms and entertainment and recreation coupons.

Effective organization is the key to sanity when using coupons. I've seen three different ways to organize them so they can be carried with you on shopping trips.

Totes – About the size of a photo box, these totes often have handles and can be carried on your shopping trips. Use simple index cards with tabs to separate coupons into categories.

I like this idea because of the ease of transport and the amount of coupons it could hold. However, it doesn't fit inside a purse.

Binders – Three-ring binders can be filled with page protectors made for baseball cards or scrapbook stickers. Coupons can be categorized and stored using the pockets.

This option isn't for me. The binder doesn't have a handle nor does it fit into a purse. Double-whammy.

Accordion Files – I use a couple of small accordion files to organize and store my coupons. Often they aren't already labeled, so I have control over that, and they're small enough to transport in a purse. This is important to me because I've had a friend or two leave them on the top of a shopping cart when they left the store; this, and I run the risk of sounding dramatic, is one of my personal nightmares.

Labeling

To begin with, I had very basic labels, and these worked for me for a long time. They were:

*Dairy
*Condiments
*Cereal
*Frozen Food
*Meat
*Drinks
*Paper Products
*Cleaning Products
*Health and Beauty
*Snacks
*Desserts

Whatever labels you choose, make sure they make sense to you. It can be quite frustrating to know that you have a coupon and then not be able to find it!

But I Have So Many Coupons...

Filing is even more important when you've collected an impressive amount of coupons. If you don't want to cut out every single coupon and file it, cut out the ones you want to carry with you – I have my favorites, like cereal and yogurt coupons. Write the date on the front cover of the ads that contain the coupons you haven't cut out. File the ads in a manila folder, envelope or drawer by date. This way, if you come across a really good deal but didn't cut out the coupon, you can go back and get it.

> *How do you remember what manufacturer coupons are in your files?*
> *DON'T!*
> *Go to Sunday Coupon Preview (.com) where you can view coupon inserts by date or do a search to find if there's been a coupon recently issued.*

My organization labels have become more refined, especially since I have two different accordion files. I also use my own kind of shorthand and abbreviations – those filing labels are pretty small!

Grocery Store File
*Breakfast items
*Yogurt
*Other Dairy
*Bread (I include the Pillsbury bread coupons in this one)
*Meat and Frozen Food
*Soups, Canned/Frozen Veggies and Fruit, Pasta Sauce
*Cooking and Baking
*Condiments
*Drinks
*Bars (Nutrigrain, Fiber One, etc.)
*Popcorn
*Snacks
*Candy, Cookies, other dessert items

Drug Store File
*Ziploc/Garbage bags, foil, plastic wrap
*Lightbulbs, batteries
*First Aid, Vitamins, Feminine Stuff
*Makeup, Hair, Deodorant, Soap
*Toothpaste, Toothbrushes, Floss, Mouthwash
*Dusting, Dishes, Air Quality (Items like Febreze, Glade, etc.)
*Paper Products – towels, toilet paper, tissue, plates
*General Cleaning
**Baby Stuff would go in this file if I collected coupons for those products.*

Sometimes a drug store will have a great sale on a food item, so I either work hard to make sure I have the food coupons I need with me beforehand, or I carry both accordion files just in case.

> *Expired coupons? Don't throw them away! Send them to the Overseas Coupon Program for military families to use. Go to www.ocpnet.org/ for more information.*

Before You Get to the Store

I like to refine my planning even further to make my trip to the grocery store as stress-free as possible. First I collect the store coupons and start a list of what products and how many of each I want to purchase. Then I find manufacturer coupons that fit with the store coupons, in my accordion files and Sunday Coupon Preview (www.SundayCouponPreview.com) to do a quick search for the manufacturer coupons I'm looking for. I make a note of any Register Rewards, Single Check Rebates, or other rebates I can take advantage of as well.

The list and the coupons go into a regular-sized envelope marked with the store's name. I put this with my accordion files in a small canvas bag and head to the store. Then I have a focused list with coupons ready to go, along with my coupon stash in case I see an unexpected deal while I'm out and about.

Overall, you'll get to know the coupons you have. Regardless, choose a labeling system that will help you. Little is worse in this process than not being able to find a coupon that you *know* you have!

How Much Should I Spend?

This is a common question, and one that's a little difficult to answer by specific product or service. I have two categories that I keep in mind while I'm couponing and shopping – the *Acceptable Price* and the *Goal Price*.

The *Acceptable Price* is what I know from experience as a pretty good price overall. Sometimes there's a store sale on a product that doesn't currently have a manufacturer coupon so I can't employ the Trifecta; however, the product isn't likely to go on sale again for awhile, or manufacturer coupons aren't produced for this specific product. If the product is at an Acceptable Price and it's on my needs list, I go ahead and purchase it.

The *Goal Price* category concerns what prices I *know* I've gotten on certain products in my history of couponing (and have therefore impressed myself, bragging to anyone who will listen regarding how little I spent). Those prices don't come along often, but they can always be a goal, especially when I'm working to use the Trifecta as much as possible.

Of course, I want as many items as possible to be FREE. The reality is that there are many items that you can regularly "purchase" for free, including toothpaste and dishwashing liquid. When these opportunities arise, don't pass them up! Make them apart of your own personal Goal Price.

If you don't have much experience with couponing, it can be difficult to know for awhile what's really a good deal or not. I've included the following chart to help with some of the specifics.

This chart is available as a free printable at www.WilsonWrites.com

Product	Acceptable Price	Goal Price*
Apples, oranges per pound	$.89	$.68
Baby carrots, per pound	$1.25	$.99
Bacon, per pound	$1.99	$1.50
Bananas per pound	$.59	$.33 - $.49
Bread (whole wheat), one loaf	$1.50	$.49
Broccoli, per pound	$.99	$.78
Brownie Mix, Cake mix	$.99	$.49
Canned soup, per can	$.89	$.49
Cereal, per box	$1	$.50
Cheese, 2 pound block	$4.49	$3.99
Cheese, shredded, per pound	$2.49	$1.90
Chicken Breasts, per pound	$2	$1.79
Chips, per bag	$1.99	$1.69
Coffee, per pound	$4	$2.49
Crackers, per box	$1	$.50

Cream cheese, 8 ounces	$1.29	$.49
Dips and Dressings	$2 each	$1each
Dish detergent, per bottle	$.99	FREE
Eggs – per dozen	$1.49	$.99
Flour tortillas, per package	$1.99	$.99
Ground Beef, per pound	$2.49	$1.49
Gum and Mints	$.49	FREE
Ice cream, per gallon	$2.49	$1.25
Juice, 64 ounces	$1.49	$.99
Ketchup, Mustard	$.99 each	$.49 each
Lean Pockets	$1.78	$1.28
Lettuce, one bunch	$1.29	$.79
Mac & Cheese, Kraft	$.79 each	$.50 each
Mayonnaise	$2.49	$1.49
Microwave Popcorn, box of 3	$1	$.49
Milk, one gallon	$1.99	1.49
Peanut butter, 18 ounces	$1.50	$.49
Razor	$3	$.99
Refried beans, per can	$.99	$.79 or less
Shrimp, one pound	$4.99 to 5.99	$3.99

Soda – 12 pack	$3	$2.25 or less
Soda – 2 liter bottle	$.99	$.49
Sour Cream, 16 ounces	$1.29	$.89
Toilet Paper, 4-pack	$1.68 (about $.42 a roll)	$.35**
Toothpaste and Toothbrushes	$.50 each	FREE
Vegetables, Canned	$.79 each	$.59 each
Vegetables, Frozen	$1.29 a pound	$.88 a pound
Yogurt, 6 ounces	$.45 each	$.30 each

*The Goal Prices have an unstated "Or Less" tacked on to the end
**One time, I did actually get a few 4-packs of toilet paper for $.35, which equals about $.09 a roll.

Are Clearance Prices Really Good Deals?

Finding those special colored stickers makes my heart-rate increase with excitement. What I've found, however, is that clearance prices often aren't as good a deal as I've previously believed.

Sometimes the markdowns aren't as deep as I feel they need to be in order to get a good deal. Usually discounts need to be 50% or more for me to consider them, and I'm impatient with anything less. Just recently, I saw a clearance sticker on a product (regular price $4 to $5) that had only been marked down $.60! That's a blatant misuse of the clearance sticker.

This also became an issue for me when I started couponing and looking for deals in the meat section of grocery stores. I determine a good deal on meat products by calculating price per pound, and I soon discovered that some of the clearance products were more expensive per pound than those on sale. Now when I peruse the clearance bins around the store, I compare the prices to the already low sale prices.

In addition, I consider whether or not I could employ the Trifecta. Sometimes I can get the same products on a sale, using store and manufacturer coupons, for less than a clearance price of 50%. Also, a clearance price may not be final. Christmas products go on discount for 50%, then 75% and finally 90%. The downside is that if you wait out the discount cycle, you're taking your chances with *not* getting something you'd either use or want.

Sometimes you don't have to wait out the discount cycle, you could just ask. When my husband decided he wanted a new watch, he shopped the clearance section at a local department store. He found a watch he wanted and used his store coupon, and the clerk was nice enough to tell him that the discount would be deeper the following day. The calculations with the clearance price, the store promotion, and the coupon were confusing, so the clerk decided to run it through the cash register's system.

As she did, my husband saw the phrase "30-day low" on the screen and asked about it. The clerk told him that items often go on a discount during a 30-day period, and this is when these products are at their lowest prices. Of course, he asked when the 30-day low would be for his watch, and she said the next day – this is when he went back to purchase it with his coupon.

Final price for his $200 watch? $30.

It pays to ask. Especially if something is on clearance, ask if there are going to be further discounts in the near future. It might pay to wait!

Building Scenarios

Building money-saving scenarios that involve the Trifecta - the combination of store sales, store coupons, and manufacturer coupons – is one of the most fun parts about couponing.

Scenarios are strategies for getting the absolute lowest price on a product or a combination of products. In the coupon world, they're called _scenarios_ with the disclaimer YMMV (Your Mileage May Vary) because, quite frankly, there's a possibility that the one you're trying may not work out.

So why try? Because you can get stuff for FREE or cheap. And I've found that most of the time, I experience success.

Setting Up the Scenario

First, scenarios are usually built on store specials or coupons, or a combination of the two. The example I'm going to use involves cereal at $1.50 a box, but only if you buy four. The ad should list which kinds and sizes qualify. There may be a store coupon for this deal, or it may just be in the ad. Either way, clip the store coupon or carry the ad with you to the store.

Then dig out *any* manufacturer coupons that will work with the cereals involved in this deal. You may get there and find that there are only two of your favorite kinds and you'll have to pick two other types of cereal to complete the deal. Or some of the coupons may be better than others depending on what you buy. Let's say for this example that you have two manufacturer coupons that state "$1 off two boxes."

This brings the four boxes of cereal down to $4 – this is pretty good. However, what would make it a great scenario is if you paid the $4 for the cereal and received a catalina for a free gallon of milk or something similar, which might make it worthwhile. But for only the cereal, the price could be lower.

The use of the store's double coupons would help. Let's say that using double coupons gets another $1 shaved off the bill. That's four boxes of cereal for $3, which is awesome considering one of these boxes at regular price is *over* $3. On paper, the scenario would look like this:

4 Boxes of cereal for $6
Minus two $1/2 manufacturer coupons (- $2)
Minus two double coupons at $.50 each (- $1)
Total OOP - $3!

Practicing Scenarios

Completing transactions involving a scenario can feel a little stressful when you first start. The cash register might beep, or the cashier is studying your coupons like they hold the keys to the meaning of life. And

When is a good time to practice?
At night, usually after the dinner hour. Cashiers and managers tend to be more friendly and helpful.

many times, successful scenarios involve completing more than one transaction.

Practicing building and completing scenarios really does help. Like with couponing, start small. Do only one tricky combination per shopping trip. Do everything in one transaction at first. Then, when you're ready - and you'll know when you're ready – plan on fitting in three or four scenarios into your outing, or split up your purchase into two transactions for maximum savings.

As you experience success, the nervousness will fade away, and completing them will be easier. It will be hard to wait for the next one you want to try!

Don't Reinvent Scenarios

As you begin practicing building and completing scenarios, recognizing the opportunities for them will become easier and more natural. Look at the ads, take note of store specials and coupons, dig for manufacturer coupons, take note of doubles and then put it all together.

It's a bit of work. I love contributing scenarios on my blog when I can, but generally I don't have the time to make up many per week. There are a few good sources for scenarios, and they usually involve friends or blogs.

Blogs

A good friend of mine referred me to my first money-saving blog. I have found that people who want to save money are family-oriented with a desire to live debt-free. They are also generous with information and strategies. Money-saving blogs are also places to get to know other people as well as share your own tips and problems, ask questions, and get help.

. Many times, the information across money-saving blogs are similar, especially if they're reporting on daily deals or freebies. However, there is an advantage to following a variety of bloggers. Different bloggers focus on different aspects of money-saving. For example, one blogger I know of regularly posts about deals at Amazon. Other bloggers tirelessly make store lists, while still others find and post the best coupons when they're released.

It is standard for bloggers to cite where they saw certain deals or posts on other websites. When you begin to read money-saving blogs and notice the citations, you'll have access to more bloggers and styles of posts.

Making Use of the Blogs

Keeping track of blogs or using the computer to find deals can feel intimidating. Truthfully, it's easy once you learn, and those skills transfer to other uses of your computer.

When I first began subscribing to blogs that I liked, I was quickly overwhelmed. I lost a blog address and couldn't find it, or I would forget to check one of the blogs so I would miss out on a deal. I needed one place where I could stay informed regarding updates on these blogs.

There is an easy way to keep up using **RSS feeds**. RSS stands for Really Simple Syndication and provides blog updates in one spot, called a reading platform. When you visit a website, you can usually find this icon on the homepage or in your browser's address bar. Click on it and that blog or website will be added to your reading platform.

My reading platform is **Google Reader** (http://www.google.com/reader). There are many more reading platforms, but I chose Google because it's easy to use. You can read more about RSS Feeds at http://www.whatisrss.com/.

If you don't want to set up an RSS feed reader, many blogs and websites have email subscriptions. I actually started out with email subscriptions and found the amount of email too overwhelming; many blogs are updated several times a day. As my interest in blogs grew, so did my interest in Google Reader. Luckily, at the bottom of each subscription email was an RSS icon, so I was able to switch to RSS pretty fast.

There are blogs – like mine, at **www.WilsonWrites.com** or **www.LiveCheapandFree.com** – that update daily with deals that have value across the country. However, local blogs are quite useful. Check to see if there are any blogs for your community or region – I'd bet money there are. The local aspect helps the blog community stay current on store specials and practices that are specific to your area.

Coupons Everywhere!

One thing I've discovered while clipping, printing and loading coupons onto my store cards:

Coupons   lead   to   more coupons!

> *Want more access? Create email addresses for other household members, and then sign them up for stuff too.*

Sign up!

If you want a bunch of cheap and free things, you're going to be signing up at a lot of websites. **Create an email address** just for this purpose.

The first reason is that your email will be more streamlined, not mixing this coupon business with your personal email. The next reason is that you will start getting email from Nigerian princes and others who request your Western Union services. A lot. Spam is easier to manage when it's not connected to your personal email address.

Another useful tool is the Google toolbar (http://toolbar.google.com/).

Install it on your browser and then use the **Autofill** feature. Whenever you come upon a registration form, click on Autofill and it will plug in your name, address, and email address for you. It saves a lot of time!

Internet Printable Coupons

There was a time that Internet Printable Coupons were difficult to use because stores didn't want to accept them. This, fortunately, is no longer the case.

Internet Printable Coupons are legitimate except when they seem too good to be true, like the "Free Pepsi 12-Pack" printable coupon going around awhile ago. You can get in trouble passing these fraudulent coupons, and fortunately store employees are aware of them just in case.

An important aspect of Internet Printable Coupons is that there are print limits. Redplum is a popular site for printable coupons, and these have overall coupon limits set for each available coupon. Once a coupon has been printed the maximum number of times, it becomes unavailable. So when you see a great coupon that you know you will use, print it!

If you don't have a good printer, now is the time to get one. You'll save far more money on groceries than you'll spend on ink (there are deals for refilling ink cartridges too), plus you can print in draft or grayscale to save in that area.

A note about printing internet coupons: **make sure your printer is hooked up to your computer at the time of printing**! Since I have a laptop, I often send items to the print queue. Then I go down to my office and print a bunch of documents at once. This is a great system; however, it doesn't work with Internet Printable Coupons.

Sometimes after you've printed a coupon, you can hit the browser's back button two to three times and print the coupon again. Rarely has this worked more than two times *per coupon* for me. If the internet printable coupon is in PDF form, that is an extra bonus since these can be downloaded and printed in an unlimited number.

Here is a list of websites that offer printable coupons; in no way is this an exhaustive list. There are many other sites, I'm sure, but I've included the ones most familiar to me.

Safeway (http://www.safeway.com/)

Target (http://www.target.com) Scroll down to the bottom to find the link to Grocery Coupons

We Use Coupons (http://www.weusecoupons.com/)

Coupons.com (http://print.coupons.com/)

Smart Source (http://coupons.smartsource.com/)

Red Plum (http://www.redplum.com/)

eclip (http://www.eclip.com/)

Shortcuts (http://www.shortcuts.com)

eCoupons

Coupons that you load onto your store loyalty cards are called eCoupons. As you peruse this list of printable coupons, check to see if there's a way to *load coupons onto your store cards*. There are a couple of companies that already offer this service. These are:

- Cellfire (www.cellfire.com)
- Shortcuts (www.shortcuts.com)

A number of grocery stores offer the use of eCoupons along with the above two services. Safeway and Fred Meyer offer eCoupons you can load onto your loyalty cards through their own websites. It's worth a look on your favorite grocery store's website before heading out.

My experience has been that these eCoupons can be combined with manufacturer and store coupons. For example, if Yoplait yogurt is on store special for forty cents each when you buy ten, the eCoupons loaded onto the store card will come off the bill *first*, then whatever paper manufacturer coupons you hand over. Then the double coupons are applied, and then you've got some cheap yogurt!

Corporate Websites

Take your Autofill capability for a spin with these **corporate websites.** When you register, you'll have access to both printable and hardcopy coupons through the mail. Some offer free samples of products, contests, sweepstakes, and free gifts. They'll probably have opportunities to sign up for newsletters, for which you now have a special email address just for that purpose. I like the newsletters because often they are accompanied by additional coupons.

Here is a list of these corporate websites:

Right @ Home (http://www.rightathome.com/)

Betty Crocker (http://www.bettycrocker.com/)

Pillsbury (http://www.pillsbury.com/)

Eat Better America (http://www.eatbetteramerica.com/)

Box Tops (http://www.boxtops4education.com/)

General Mills – search the particular brand, such as

"General Mills, Cheerios"

Purchasing Coupons

Searching for internet printable coupons for specific items that you want alleviates some of the need for purchasing coupons. When you pay

> *On Ebay, you can search for the specific coupon you want. Then you have the option to "Buy it Now."*

for coupons, you're actually paying for another person to find, clip and send you the coupons, not the coupons themselves.

A few of the services that provide clipped coupons are The *Coupon Clippers* (http://www.thecouponclippers.com/) and The *Coupon Master* (http://www.thecouponmaster.com/). Another source to purchase coupons is *EBay* (http://www.ebay.com/), and if you use a *referral website*, you could earn extra points or cash back.

If you order coupons from one seller, you save on postage; generally 10 to 20 coupons should cost $1 to $2. If you buy coupons from more than one seller, it will cost a bit more. Make sure you choose coupons with a high enough value for your effort – for example, $.55 on two packages of granola bars isn't as good as $1 on two.

More Places to Find Coupons

Coupons lead to more coupons as well as a variety of places to find them.

- **Requesting Coupons** – many consumers have had great success with receiving coupons from companies that produce the products they love to use or want to try. How? One way is to request a coupon or a sample of a product (if you haven't used it but want to try it). Another way is to bring an issue to the attention of the corporate office (in other words, a valid complaint). A kinder strategy is to offer a helpful suggestion or a sincere, personal compliment about a product.

- **Magazine Subscriptions** – Once you start bargain hunting, you'll discover deeply discounted or free subscriptions to popular magazines. Inside these magazines? Coupons.

- **Blinkies** – Have you passed through an aisle at the grocery store and noticed a red blinking light? This belongs to a coupon dispenser, which is called a "Blinkie." Grab a few of these coupons as you pass by and file them away for later use.

- **Peelies** – These coupons are attached to products with an amazingly strong adhesive, and if you're skillful and lucky, you can peel off the coupon without destroying the product's packaging. Grab and file these coupons!

- **Tear Pads** – These coupons are similar to peelies, only they're not located on the products, but on a pad near the products. Usually they can be found on special displays. They are highly coveted because they usually have extremely long expiration dates and tend to be higher value. The holiday season during November and December traditionally bring out the largest volume of tear pad coupons.

What About Natural Products?

Grocery stores focused on natural and organic products accept coupons, and there are also special online resources to find coupons for natural and organic products.

- Delicious Living (http://deliciouslivingmag.com/ - click *coupons* tab)
- Health E Savers (http://www.healthesavers.com/HealthESavers/Coupons.aspx)
- Horizon Organic (http://www.horizondairy.com/ - click coupons tab on the top left)
- Kiwi (http://www.kiwimagonline.com/ecoupons/)
- Mambo Sprouts (http://www.mambosprouts.com/coupons/)
- Organic Valley Coupons (http://www.organicvalley.coop/coupons/)
- Stonyfield Farms (http://www.stonyfield.com/register/ - register to receive coupons)

Rebates

Rebates are a great way to get even more savings from your couponing strategies, but it requires a little bit of organization. Find a place to keep drug store and grocery store receipts, usually for about 2 to 3 months. I have found that rebates crop up, and more often than not, I've already bought the required items. I almost missed out on one rebate, so now I keep a stash of receipts to hunt through should I need one for a rebate.

There's also the issue of buying specifically for a rebate. **Read the restrictions** carefully. There's usually a timeframe, a dollar requirement, and a "same purchase" rule, meaning that all of the items included in the rebate have to be purchased together. Also, you'll need to figure out how to use your coupons in order to get the lowest prices on the items when you buy them in order to take full advantage of the rebate.

At the back of the book (Appendix J) is a Rebate Tracking Sheet. This is a form to keep track of what rebates you've sent and when, as well as when you might get a response.

It's always a good idea to photocopy forms and receipts before you send them, and carefully read the instructions for redemption. Sometimes the company will send an incomplete rebate submission back to you to complete, but they can just as easily toss it in the trash or recycle bin.

It's also fun to have a special purpose for your rebate checks. I deposit mine into a special savings account that I use for Christmas shopping or special extras, like a summer trip to the beach for my family. However you use the money, I'm sure it will be welcome!

Use this Rebate Tracking Sheet to keep track of your rebates, downloadable on www.WilsonWrites.com!

Product/Item or Company	Rebate Amount	Date Submitted	Approximate Response Time	Date Rebate Received

Prescription Rolling

If you have a few prescriptions in your family's arsenal, make them work for you. Rolling prescriptions is moving them from one pharmacy to another in order to take advantage of a store's gift card promotion.

For example, there are many store-specific coupons that reward a gift card of a specified amount when a prescription is **transferred** to their

> *Read the fine print on prescription transfer coupons and gift card promotions.*

pharmacy. Rarer are the **new prescription** coupons – when you see them, grab them! If you have kids, it's likely you'll get a new prescription (whether from illness or fluoride) before the expiration date on the coupon, and then you can get a gift card. The coupons are found in the store's ads or sometimes online at a store's website.

Some pharmacies have time limits regarding prescription coupons. One drug store I've gone to states that one coupon per person within a six month time period. Now's the time to use that calendar! Mark six months from when you use the coupon and note the store and person whose prescription was used. Then you'll know when you can roll a prescription again at that store using that person's name/prescription.

Seem confusing? It sounds more confusing than it actually is. Remember, it's all about **organization**. In that spirit, <u>Appendix H</u> is a spreadsheet to help you keep track of rolling prescriptions.

Prescription Owner	Current Prescription Location	Rolling Date and Location Is there a time limit?	Next Rolling Location and Approximate Date

Referral Services

Some people are hesitant to shop online because they have to use a credit card to complete purchases. I personally don't have a credit card, so that means I'd have to use my debit card, and I'm not comfortable with that either.

A couple of options for online shopping include opening another bank account, putting some money in it specifically for online shopping, and using _that_ debit card for online purchases. That way, if anything should happen, it wouldn't affect your main account.

Another option is to use _Paypal_ (https://www.paypal.com/). It's password protected and hooked to a checking account, but you use the service to buy and sell items without having to mess with credit or debit card numbers. You could still open a separate bank account to use with Paypal as well.

When you decide how to pay for online purchases, check out a **referral service** in order to get something back. Referral Services are websites that maintain point systems or offer a percentage back when you use their websites to make purchases.

These are good places to use your separate email address that

you opened to use with couponing. Many of these also offer

referral bonuses.

- **Swag Bucks** – (http://swagbucks.com/) Use this site to search the web and get paid in "Swagbucks" redeemable for items through their website.

- **My Points** – (http://www.mypoints.com/) Earn points by reading email and making purchases. Redeem points for gift cards.

- **Inbox Dollars** – (http://www.inboxdollars.com/) Get paid to read emails, take surveys and complete offers. Instead of points, in accumulating cash. When you reach $30 in earnings, you can request a check.

- **Ebates** – (http://www.ebates.com/) Offers a percentage back based on the retailer and amount of purchase. Money accumulates over three months, and then is reviewed. If the amount of cash is more than $10, Ebates sends a check.

Make sure you sign in through the referral website and use it to search or purchase items. Otherwise, your purchase won't count toward your reward.

There are also **coupon codes** that corporations or stores release that can often discount your purchase or allow free shipping. Coupon codes are entered during the checkout process, usually near the spot for gift certificate redemption.

There are websites that keep track of these codes and allow you to look them up by store name or by the item you wish to purchase. They also keep track of other web deals to the consumer's benefit.

My favorite coupon code websites are:

- **Deals.com** (http://www.deals.com/)

- **Current Codes** (http://www.currentcodes.com/)

- **Retail Me Not** (http://www.retailmenot.com/)

In order to get the best deal, I **combine a referral service with a coupon code** to make online purchases. Usually the coupon code will at least cover the cost of shipping, if not a little more. This is worth the sanity I save by being able to shop at home!

Surveys

Some couponers are really into surveys and can earn good rewards by working with survey companies. I've tried them and found that I didn't have the patience for them. Because of that, I don't personally know if they're worth completing, but I have read that they are.

Plus, surveys – like many online "opportunities"- can be ill-disguised scams. I ran across the website **ScamBusters** (http://www.scambusters.org/), and they seem to have pretty good information on what to look for in a reputable survey site.

Some of the more popular survey sites are:

- **Survey Spot** (http://surveyspot.com/)

- **Ipsos i-say** – (http://www.i-say.com/) complete surveys and earn points to redeem for gift cards

- **Valued Opinions** – (http://www.valuedopinions.com/) Completed surveys pay $2 to $5, stored in your account until accumulated total is $20. Then redeem for gift certificates.

- **Opinion Outpost** – (https://www.opinionoutpost.com/) Surveys pay in points, 10 points equals $1.

The Social Shopping Phenomenon

During the past couple of years, there's been an insurgence of an experience called Social Shopping, and there are great deals to be had. These Social Shopping sites work with local businesses to offer products and services to those who sign up to buy them for one day only. If enough people elect to buy the product, then the deal is honored.

These Social Shopping sites include Groupon, BuyWithMe and Living Social, along with others that are local to certain areas, like Portland Daily Deals. The basics of these sites include:

- One deal a day at a great price
- A group buying experience where the deal is "On" if enough people buy it
- The websites are easy to navigate
- A focus on businesses local to you

There are definitely advantages to using Social Shopping sites. One is that the deals are local, which supports your community's economy. Another is that you can get great deals on products and services you use anyway – I got half-off carpet cleaning for my house, and I've been able to purchase other offers as gifts.

One of the disadvantages is that the deals are available for one day only, and if you are an impulsive shopper at all, then this situation might not be one you want to mess with. For me, there have been a few temptations I've had to refuse based on budget considerations.

Other than that, there are great deals in the Social Shopping experience to help save money on gifts, products and services in your city!

Down on the Farm

Use your savings from couponing to feed your family healthy, natural and local food using the following resources.

The Growing Popularity of CSAs

A couple of years ago, I read an article about Community Supported Agriculture (CSA) in my area. A CSA is a farm where people - called "shareholders" - pledge money for a season at a local farm and then receive a share of the produce during the harvest.

I signed up right away with Birds and Bees Community Farm, where I was on a waiting list for two years. It was well worth the wait. Our share provides fresh food from Birds and Bees every other week that includes food like lettuce, beets, garlic curls, spearmint, farm-fresh eggs, 2 pints of Oregon strawberries, a small container of raspberries, a variety of other salad greens, a couple of carrots, an onion, a cucumber, and radishes. The harvest specifics change each week, but it's always fresh and delicious.

To find out more about CSAs in your area, do an internet search for "Community Supported Agriculture, (your city), (your state)." They are growing in popularity, so chances are you'll find one and at least get started on a waiting list.

Local, Grass-Fed Meat

Another popular practice is to buy grass-fed meat from farmers in your local area. Purchasing meat this way supports the local economy and helps maintain your family's health and safety.

There are a variety of options to buying beef, pork and chicken products this way, from having smaller portions cut and packaged for pick-up to buying part of a cow to get butchered and stored to eat during the year. It will cost more, but one of the reasons I use my money-saving strategies for other products is to be able to buy this kind of meat.

Farm and Produce Stands

There's probably at least one Farm or Produce Stand in your area that offers locally grown, organic food at reasonable prices. Instead of buying produce at a grocery store, consider seeking out one of these local markets to support economically. I've found that the fruit and vegetables are fresher and worth the extra pennies each week. Plus, you may be able to get well-priced organic dairy products, eggs and bread as well.

Farmer's Markets

Farmer's Markets are great places to buy fresh, local food during the spring and summer months. The popularity for Farmer's Markets has grown dramatically over the last few years, and there are many available throughout greater metropolitan areas. Each town's Farmers Market operates during specific days and times during the week, with a wide variety of offerings depending on which ones you visit. No matter where you go, the price for this often organic and all-natural food is worth it!

Top Three Ways to Shop Thrift Stores

Thrift stores are great places to find a variety of items at great prices.

Find Them

Use the Thrift Store Spreadsheet (*Appendix F*) as you find and shop **local thrift stores**. Some of my favorite thrift stores are in my neighborhood. One of the ways to find them is to look in ads that specialize in advertising local businesses. One of the "gently used" clothing stores in my area even puts coupons in the local ads, which compounds potential savings.

Shopping local helps your community!

I have done internet searches for thrift stores in my area, but nothing can replace taking a drive, noting any stores that have the words *thrift, bargain, outlet* or any form of *liquidator/liquidation* in their titles.

Analyze Each Store

The only way to know if you're getting a good deal based on what you're looking for is to take time to check them out. Some thrift stores have better selections or prices than others, and I've seen more local thrift stores that specialize in specific kinds of items.

There are thrift stores that are well-known, like Goodwill, Value Village, the Salvation Army and Deseret Industries. I've noticed that their prices tend to be a little higher, but I've gotten some good deals. The only way to know for certain is to shop around, take notes, and compare them with local stores.

Know the Pitfalls

There's a variety of possible pitfalls when doing business at a thrift store. Some stores only take cash, and it's sad to arrive at the cash register and realize that you have none. Another issue involves being able to return items with a receipt – some will do only immediate exchanges, certain stores will refund money, and others state that all sales are final. It's important to be clear on the

store's policies before making a purchase.

Use this sheet (found in Appendix F) to take notes on thrift stores in your community.

Name of Thriftstore/ Location	Take Coupons/ Have own coupons?	Rewards Program?	Clothing? Housewares? Grocery?	Other Notes

The Value in Shopping the Outlets

There are, however, some items you probably don't want to buy at thrift stores, like socks. Underwear. That kind of stuff. For those items, I head to the closest **outlet stores**.

If you look up these outlet stores online, you can sign up for coupons and discounts, which can be combined with stores' clearance prices or special sales. And outlet stores often use their own system of rewards; I have cards from Bali, Jockey, Eddie Bauer, and Van Heusen, to name a few. The store rewards systems get me extra coupons and percentages off my purchases on top of the outlet-sponsored coupons. Usually items at outlets are already offered at a much discounted price, and the coupons will make your deals even sweeter.

Those deals in outlet stores probably involve items that are out of season. For example, they have summer clothes at great prices in the fall. This is a great way to buy clothes, even for growing children; buy them a size or two larger than they need.

Another way to shop out of season is to wander the aisles of the stores you already frequent. If I need to go to Fred Meyer or Target because I have a coupon for milk, I take an extra ten minutes or so to browse the various clearance sections. I have found some fun Halloween stuff in December and Valentine's decorations in March for up to 75% off. Plus, I've gotten out of the house for an additional ten minutes and haven't made an extra trip!

Household Savings

It's not easy to make cuts to your budget, especially concerning necessities. You probably could cut out electricity, gas, and phone bills, but it may not be realistic (especially in the winter). Instead, it's a good use of time to see if you can lower any of these common household bills.

Insurance

If it's been awhile, get some new insurance quotes from comparison websites. Use referral websites, such as My Points, to see if you can earn some points or money by completing the comparisons. Don't be afraid to switch companies if you can save some money.

- **Accuquote** (http://www.accuquote.com/) – Good for Life Insurance quotes. Don't have life insurance? Get some!

- **Your Online Quote** (http://youronlinequote.com/) – Good for Home Insurance quotes.

- **NetQuote** – (http://www.netquote.com/) Car Insurance company comparisons.

Energy Use

This is a good time to evaluate your home. When gas and food prices started to rise over the last couple of years, we decided we needed to cut costs, but we had no idea where to start on the home front.

My husband had heard about the **Energy Trust of Oregon** (http://www.energytrust.org/), a company with the sole purpose of helping people save energy. A representative came to our house and helped identify areas where we could cut energy costs. They also gave us free products to get started, such as water-saving shower heads and compact fluorescents.

If you don't live in Oregon, find out if your state has a similar program. If not, request a consultation from your energy company. In the Pacific Northwest, these are:

- Portland General Electric

    (http://www.portlandgeneral.com/default.aspx)

- Pacific Power (http://www.pacificpower.net/)

- Northwest Natural Gas

  (https://www.nwnatural.com/index.asp)

- Cascade Natural Gas (http://www.cngc.com/)

Many **energy companies also offer classes** to community residents and businesses in order to help save energy and money.

Seasonal bills can be hard on the wallet. Heating costs rise in winter, sometimes making those bills difficult to pay. Energy companies often have programs to help even out those seasonal differences.

> *Check with your local Home Depot about recycling compact fluorescents.*

One of those programs is called **Equal Pay**. This program is available for customers who have been with the utility company for 12 months or more. The average monthly bill per is calculated based on your household's past usage. Equal pay accounts are reviewed every 12 months and the monthly payment is adjusted for the next 12 months. If the year was overpaid or underpaid, that is calculated into the next year's payments.

If you haven't been with your utility company for 12 months, there is a program called **Average Pay**. In this program, the monthly bill is adjusted to reflect the most recent average use and evens out the seasonal highs and lows. Then, after 12 months, you could enroll in Equal Pay.

For the long-term, check your furnace for repair or replacement. There are also rebates and grants for energy conservation improvements. You can check them here (http://www.dsireusa.org/) by state. Also, **House Energy** (http://www.house-energy.com/) is a great resource to research other ways to save energy and money around the house.

Easy Ways to Cut Electrical Costs

Strategies that you can implement immediately include:

- Use a programmable thermostat, setting it to 68 degrees in winter and 78 degrees in summer

- Insulate your home well, including caulk and weather stripping

- Use heavy drapes to help control the temperature of your home

- Unplug appliances that aren't being used

- Put up storm windows or weatherproof with plastic in the winter

- Do laundry less often, and line-dry your clothes

These tips require a little more time, but save valuable funds in everyday life!

Internet, Phone and Cable TV

Initially, we bundled our internet, phone and cable services due to a low introductory rate. After about six months, the low rate was gone and the cost kept rising from month to month.

> *Get a "no"? Keep asking. If you try to negotiate for a better deal, price, or payment option and receive an automatic "no", ask for a supervisor. Keep doing this until you make progress. It may take a while, but it's worth it.*

My husband devoted an hour on the phone one night to negotiate a lower rate or to see how the plan could be changed in order for us to save some money. The company was willing to negotiate, and we are now happy with our payment for their services.

There are referral websites out there that will help you compare rates and services from cable companies as well as satellite networks. Two of these include **Whitefence** (http://www.whitefence.com/) and **Connect My Cable** (http://www.connectmycable.com/).

Cell Phones

Few things irritate me more than a Bluetooth sticking out of the side of someone's head. There's really *no way* that person could miss a phone call right now?

And, you can probably guess, I'm not a big fan of cell phones either. We had a family plan for a couple of years, and it was supposed to be $50 a month which equals $600 a year. Instead, with all of the fees and miscellaneous charges, it was $70 a month, which is $840 a year. I recently booked a week-long vacation – hotel and airfare - for my husband and myself that only cost $790, to give some perspective.

Do you really *need* a cell phone? I challenge you to go without it for one week, and aside from convenience or fun, how often do you actually *need* it? Stores and gas stations still have land-line phones, and enough of my friends have cell phones that I can borrow one if I absolutely feel the need to use one.

If you buy an unlocked phone, you'll need a SIM card for the phone company providing your pre-paid service. These cards are over $80 in stores, but only $6-$7 online.

We now think they're necessary. I disagree.

My husband, however, loves his cell phone. So, at his request, we researched ways that it would be financially justifiable for him to have one.

We discovered pre-paid plans. These plans allow consumers to purchase amounts of minutes in blocks of $25, $50 and $100. The minutes have expiration dates, and the best deal is to buy the $100 block that lasts for a year. When I use a cell phone, we buy

2 $100 blocks for each of us, which equals $400 total for the year. That's big savings.

Pre-paid plans used to be a bit sketchy concerning charges, fees and coverage areas. Now there are several different pre-paid cell phone plans from reputable companies, and websites like **Let's Talk** (http://www.letstalk.com/), **My Rate Plan** (http://www.myrateplan.com/) and **Consumer Search** (http://www.consumersearch.com/cell-phone-plans) provide comparisons of companies and rates.

Sometimes you can get a free phone with a pre-paid card that will make it even more cost effective, but those deals are rare. And my husband didn't like the phones marketed toward pre-paid users. He wanted a Blackberry, which tend to be expensive. But last year's models are cheap on Ebay and they come unlocked, which means they are ready for any service. Plus, if you use a referral website like My Points, you can earn some points with your purchase of a cell phone.

Going Green

In late winter and early spring, seed packets go on sale. I'm not suggesting you turn your yard into a full-on garden; I am, after all, known around my yard as "The Plant Killer."

Like everything else, start small. Last year I wanted to **garden** something that would live through the summer and into the fall. I found two hearty, fast-growing plants that will help feed our family: lettuce and spinach. Plant enough and you can cut them all summer, but don't forget to water them.

This summer, I'd like to get into **composting**, especially since you don't necessarily have to keep anything alive. Two websites that claim composting is easy are **Mother Earth News** (http://www.motherearthnews.com/) and **Learn2Grow** (http://www.learn2grow.com/projects/quickeasy/outdoors/quickeas ycomposting.aspx). The compost will help my lettuce and spinach thrive. Who knows? Maybe I'll try an additional crop this year.

One thing I've always wanted to try is **collecting rainwater** to use in the garden (I live in Oregon; it seems like a no-brainer).

Garden Water Saver (http://www.gardenwatersaver.com/) has instructions on how to make rain barrels for this purpose. It looks pretty cheap, and will help conserve water usage and your water bill.

If you are still getting bills in the mail, I suggest saving a tree and **receiving notices online**. Paying bills online is also easy, although there are minimal fees associated with this service. But it saves time, the paper the bill initially was printed on, the check you'd write, the envelope to send the bill back with payment, and the stamp. To me, it's worth it. If you don't want to have to remember to go online to pay bills, there's also automatic bill payment available through the companies you need to pay or through your bank.

Living in the Pacific Northwest, I've taken my curbside and can/bottle **recycling programs** for granted. I thought every community participated in these kinds of programs, and it wasn't until we vacationed in Montana that I realized otherwise. Recycling is an easy way to practice conservation, and our curbside program costs are included in our garbage bill. If you don't currently recycle in this way, the **National Recycling Coalition** (http://www.nrc-recycle.org/) keeps a directory of resources. Simply click on your state for local recycling information. According to **Green Living** (http://greenliving.lovetoknow.com/), state statistics for recycling are improving, but so much more can be done.

Cleaning Supplies

I was recently at a playgroup for my son, talking with other moms while our kids pushed each other around and fought over toys. In the midst of these squabbles, we got to talking about saving money around the house, and a few of the moms brought up cleaning supplies.

Apparently you can do quite a bit with a few cheap ingredients, including vinegar, baking soda, borax and dish detergent. And water, of course! You'll also need a couple of spray bottles.

<u>Kitchen</u> – 1 tbsp. dish detergent in a spray bottle, fill the rest with water. Another option: vinegar instead of dish detergent.

<u>Bathroom</u> – Use ½ cup borax or white vinegar in the toilet, scrub with pumice stones (use gloves, of course). Spread car wax on the toilet bowl and shower drains to keep them clean longer.

For the bathtub, use Borax or <u>Bon Ami</u> cleaner. Bon Ami seems safe enough to use on almost anything. There's a comprehensive list on their website.

For a <u>clogged drain</u>, use vinegar and baking soda.

<u>Floors</u> - Mix vinegar and water in a ratio of 1:1.

And, apparently you can make your own baby wipes, too!

One of my goals is to not have to buy chemical cleaning products again, so I've been intrigued for some time concerning steam cleaners and mops. I bought a **Shark** (for less than retail, of course) and I'm pretty happy with the power of steam. One of my favorite features is the reusable mop pads – I just throw them in the wash with my towels – while other mops on the market have disposable pads, which create more waste.

The great thing about cleaning naturally is that it doesn't have to be expensive – you can clean much of your house with water, baking soda, and vinegar!

Christmas Savings

Someone once pointed out to me that Jesus received only three gifts, so each person in their family received only three as well. I found value in this idea of setting limits for gift giving.

> _Don't just store toys and gifts for Christmas all during the year. Keep your eyes open for those great deals for birthdays, too!_

Thoughtfully preparing for the Christmas season helps maintain a measure of peace in the midst of chaos. One way to prepare is to shop **the day after Christmas**. You'll already be shopping for the _next Christmas_ season.

Compared to the day after Thanksgiving, shopping the day after Christmas is a joy. There's virtually no traffic and, if you get out early enough, no crowds.

For me, however, there is a condition: in order to take advantage of the after-Christmas sales, I need to have my Gift Spreadsheet ready (Appendix I).

Gift Spreadsheet

You can find a downloadable and printable version of this sheet at www.WilsonWrites.com!

Person/Family	Ideas/Budget	Gifts Purchased	Actual $ Spent
Family Picture			
Letters/Postage			
After Xmas Sales			

This spreadsheet lists the people for whom we'll be getting gifts, a budgeted amount to spend, a space to list what has already been purchased, and a space to list what still needs to be purchased. The spreadsheet is a terrific resource when I'm in the middle of "50%-off madness" and I need a reminder of my limits.

The spreadsheet also allows me the flexibility to purchase gifts all year, which means no frantic scurrying around the week before Christmas, vying for that last-minute gift. Because I know about what I want to spend, I can parcel it out over time, thereby saving time, money, and sanity.

Common Frugal Frustrations

Sometimes it feels like I'm all alone when I experience frustration when trying to live frugally. After connecting with other like-minded people, I've discovered that many of us have encountered similar situations. Consider this a personal heads-up from me – you're not alone!

Registering a Complaint

I've never had a cashier squeal with delight when I've handed over a pile of coupons. Overall, they aren't mean about it, but when couponing, you have to stick up for yourself.

As with most situations, just being nice goes a long way. Engage in conversation or banter. Crack a few jokes. Ask the cashier questions about his or her life. Then, if there's a question about a coupon, it may go to your advantage.

But sometimes it doesn't.

I read a story on one of my favorite blogs about a woman using coupons at a drug store. The employee claimed that the store would not accept a certain coupon. The shopper disagreed with the employee, so she whipped out her cell phone and dialed the corporate office. It turned out that the store did accept the coupon, and the person at the corporate office requested to speak to the employee in order to clear up the matter. And the shopper's coupon was honored.

Shortly after reading this story, I stopped in at a local drugstore. On every counter and ad holder was a small sign – **"We will no longer accept manufacturer internet printable coupons effective immediately**." I was curious; after all, stores are reimbursed the value of manufacturer coupons.

I asked one of the cashiers for clarification. He didn't know the reason for the new policy, and he called a manager over.

"I dunno," the manager said and shrugged.

"Well, why would this store not accept manufacturer coupons in any form, including internet printables?"

He sighed. "They're being abused." Before I could ask any more questions, he turned and walked away.

Still confused, I left the store and headed for my computer, where I wrote the corporate office an email documenting my exchange with the manager and asking that the policy in question be discontinued. Two days later, I received a phone call from the manager, apologizing and stating that they would in fact be accepting internet printable manufacturer coupons.

I was happy that the policy was changed, but it also reminded me that some fights are worth fighting, especially when it comes to saving money.

There will be situations where the cashier simply doesn't care. When I'm scouting check-out lines for cashiers, sometimes I'll choose the reluctant teenager who's just working this job to help pay their car insurance. They don't care about you and they don't care about coupons, so they'll just push them through. But watch out for accuracy – the not caring can work against you if you're not paying attention.

Which brings me to receipts. Sometimes mistakes happen, so **check your receipts immediately**. If there's a mistake, go to customer service and get it corrected right away. If it's just a couple of dollars one time and you let it go, then you get in the habit of letting it go. Pretty soon, that couple of dollars one time add up to several dollars over many small mistakes. Get in the habit of getting mistakes corrected.

I mentioned this earlier in the book, but it bears repeating. Sometimes you're going to have to register a complaint about an unsatisfactory experience with shopping with coupons. Here are some effective steps to complaining:

- Be polite. Always.

- Be informed – carry coupon policies with you and share them with the store's employees and managers, who may not know them as well as you do.

- If you need to, complain in writing using the company's complaint form online.

To register a clear complaint, use the following template:

<Greeting>

*My name is <**Your Name**> and I frequently shop at <**store name**> at <**store location**>.*

*On <**enter date and time**>, I had a problem with purchasing a product at your store. <Explain **the facts** of the problem – emotions are next.>*

*As a result of this transaction, I feel <**supply your own feeling words**>. I feel this way because <**state your reasons**>. I would like a resolution to this problem. <**This is VERY IMPORTANT – state how you want the problem to be solved to your satisfaction**>.*

*You can contact me at <**contact information here**>.*

Thanks,

*<**Your Name**>*

Many times, the response to this complaint will be in the form of an email acknowledging receipt of your complaint along with a phone call, and hopefully the problem will be resolved quickly!

Is Free Stuff Really Free?

My husband wanted a GPS, and he decided to open an account with a local bank to earn one. This bank was offering a free specific type of GPS based on the completion of requirements involving depositing money into the account, keeping a certain balance for a specified amount of time, using the debit card, and paying two bills with the account.

I'm happy to say that my husband received his GPS, but it definitely cost him, mostly in hours of his life that he can't get back. After he opened the account, there was a problem with both the deposit and the bill-pay feature, which translated to two hours on the phone, correcting and re-correcting the problem. Then the GPS they said he was supposed to get wasn't the same one that was advertised in the offer, which equaled more time on the phone.

The answer to the question "Is free stuff really free?" is… "Sometimes."

In order to get free things, there is often a commitment of time, like in my husband's case. Sometimes it's a short amount of time, like signing up for email updates or newsletters that you can later cancel.

Websites that offer free stuff require caution – some are tied to programs that require membership and/or participation. Remember when you got 6 CDs from a company for a penny, but then you had to buy three more in four years? Then, if you didn't, you'd be penalized? These "free stuff" websites are similar in theory and level of annoyance.

My Catalina Didn't Print

Catalinas are coupons that print at checkout and are handed to you with your receipt. If they don't print when you want them to

– as in store specials that offer a $10 coupon when you purchase $25 worth of specific items – the store can sometimes correct the problem.

If the store is unable to fix it, then you can call Catalina yourself at 1-888-826-8766 (choose option 3). Make sure you have your receipt in front of you in order to give them date, time and store information. They will give you directions on how to receive the coupon you're missing.

Other Frustrations

I've been couponing consistently for about five years, and I've had a variety of frustrating experiences. Some of these include:

- the deal I want to do is falling apart
- the product I want isn't in stock
- I forgot my coupons
- I can't find the coupon I want to use
- the coupon I want to use has expired or the checker won't take it

There are more, but usually the situations are spaced out well enough so that I don't get too discouraged. If you arrive at a high frustration level, take a couponing break and come back to it later. Evaluate why you coupon and what you're getting out of it. It will be worth it!

How To Get Free Beer

I like to brag that I can get free beer. There are three main ways that I do this:

- Register Rewards – this is the trickiest, since technically the Register Rewards say that they can't be used for alcohol. Like many coupon situations, it depends on the checker.

- Single Check Rebate – these rebates come in the mail from Rite Aid after you buy eligible products and submit your receipts. You can use them just like cash, and I've used them to purchase beer.

- Rolling Prescriptions – When they're available, you can use coupons that get you gift cards when you transfer prescriptions. These gift cards can be used for a variety of products, and I've used them to buy beer.

The important point of this exercise is to use money-saving strategies with products in order to get others for FREE!

Evaluate & Share

The key to living cheap and free is to communicate. Every year, my husband and I sit down and evaluate where we are financially, usually in January.

It's a good time to look back on the budget year, make adjustments and ask questions about overspending and underspending. It's a time to recommit to this process and share what we've learned. It's also a time to talk about our short-term and long-term financial goals for the coming year.

Aside from this annual meeting, budget meetings need to happen at a consistent time _each week_. Money is really easy to spend, and before you know it, you don't have any! This usually only happens to us if we're not meeting and communicating.

Communicating with others is also an important part of this process. It's my human nature to want to keep good information a secret, selfishly thinking all the good stuff will be gone if I share it with others. This is simply not true. Sharing with others multiplies the blessings I experience while blessing other people. So many of us are trapped in debt, not quite knowing how to deal with money in healthy ways. This is your chance not only to help yourself, but to help others learn to live cheap and free!

Long-Term Saving

Living cheap and free is a long-term process of saving money and practicing good stewardship. My website – **Wilson Writes** (www.wilsonwrites.com) – will continue to have tips and articles to address different aspects of this process, updated several times a week. You can sign up for convenient email updates, or this would be a perfect opportunity to break in your Google Reader account and subscribe to my RSS feed!

Don't hesitate to share your own experiences and success stories at my website as well. Encouragement helps all of us keep the momentum in this money-saving venture. As questions arise, please contact me through my website and ask. If I don't know the answer, maybe someone else does, and we can all learn together!

Appendix

Appendix A – Budget Template

Download a complete Budget Template at www.WilsonWrites.com

February 2009

Income	Budgeted	Actual
Jeff's Check		
Kelly's Check		
Gross Income		
Expenses		
Tithe & Compassion		
Life Insurance		
Investment Company		
Mortgage		
Car/Homeowners Ins.		
Gas		
Electricity		
Garbage		
Water/Sewer		
Cable/phone		
Hair Cuts		
Pet Supplies		
Copays		
Auto Rep/Maintenance		
Grocery		
Gas		
Entertainment		
Clothes		
Daycare week 1		
Daycare week 2		
Daycare week 3		
Daycare week 4		
Total Expenses		
Income minus expenses		

Appendix B – Out of Debt Sources

Get-Out-of-Debt Sources on the Web:

http://www.daveramsey.com/

http://www.crown.org/

http://www.suzeorman.com/

http://www.nfcc.org/

http://www.consumercredit.com/

*Disclaimer: I have no personal experience with the above resources, nor do I personally recommend them. They are provided for your information only.

Appendix C – Weekly Calendar

Monday	Tuesday	Wednesday	Thursday	Friday

Monday	Tuesday	Wednesday	Thursday	Friday

Monday	Tuesday	Wednesday	Thursday	Friday

Appendix D – Clean the Closets!

Location (Garage, etc.)	Items to Sell	Items to Give Away	Items to Keep

Appendix E – Analyze Spending

Budget Tracking Sheet Analysis

1. List your observations:

2. Questions:

    *Where are you underspending?

    *Where are you overspending?

    *What changes can you make? What can you cut?

Appendix F – Thirftstore Notes

Name of Thriftstore/ Location	Take Coupons/ Have own coupons?	Rewards Program?	Clothing? Housewares? Grocery?	Other Notes

Appendix G – Grocery Store Analysis

Name of Store	Ads with Store Coupons Available?	Accepts Competitors' Coupons?	Has or Accepts Double Coupons?	Rewards Program? Bag Credit?

Appendix H – Prescription Rolling

Prescription Owner	Current Prescription Location	Rolling Date and Location Is there a time limit?	Next Rolling Location and Approximate Date

Appendix I - Christmas List

Person/Family	Ideas/Budget	Gifts Purchased	Actual $ Spent
Family Picture			
Letters/Postage			
After Xmas Sales			

Appendix J – Rebate Tracking Sheet

Product/Item or Company	Rebate Amount	Date Submitted	Approximate Response Time	Date Rebate Received

Glossary

Term	Definition
Catalina	A coupon that prints out from the cash register after a transaction has been completed.
Double Coupon	Coupon issued by a store that matches the value of a coupon up to a certain amount. For example, a double coupon from Safeway matches up to $.50 of the value of a coupon.
"Food Day"	Oregon's Tuesday ads delivered to homes free of charge.
Internet Printable	A coupon printed at home from an internet source.
MC	Manufacturer Coupon, stated by the expiration date at the top of the coupon. Issued from the company that makes the product.

OOP	Out of Pocket – how much money actually spent on a transaction after coupons, rebates and gift cards.
OYNO	On Your Next Order (Purchase)
Raincheck	A form from a store when a product is out of stock. Allows customer to buy the product when it comes in at the sale or coupon price.
Rebate	Money issued to the consumer after conditions of a rebate have been met, usually by submission of a form, receipt and UPC symbol.
RR	Register Rewards are catalinas issued by Walgreen's after purchase of specific products. They are like cash for use at Walgreen's.
SC	Store Coupon, issued by a store usually through a Sunday or Tuesday ad and only accepted at that store.
Scenario	A plan to buy certain items using discounts, store and manufacturer coupons, and rebates in order to get the lowest price.

SCR	Single Check Rebate – a program operated by Rite Aid. Submit receipts each month for specified items (online or through the mail) and request the rebate at the end of the period. *Rebate can only be processed once each period.*
Stack	The strategy of combining store specials, store coupons and manufacturer coupons for maximum savings on products.
Transaction	Where money is exchanged for products.
UPC	Symbol found on products, usually in barcode form.
YMMV	An abbreviation for "Your Mileage May Vary," which refers to the possibility that the possible deal might not work out the same for one person as another.

Acknowledgements

The first edition of this book brought along with it many new and fun experiences, and I'm really happy to have the chance to write a second edition. I want to appreciate my husband, who continues to support me without fail. I thank him for getting us out of debt and then encouraging me in all of my writing endeavors

I also appreciate Jamie Young, who's an awesome and creative webmaster. Thank you also to Ruth Wallin, who looked at me during one of our conversations about saving money and said, "You know, you should really market yourself," which turned out to be great advice.

I could not do anything without my good friends Charlotte Kammer, Christine Draper and Tae-ja Griggs, who definitely make life more meaningful and fun. And thank you finally to readers and supporters of Wilson Writes as we continue on this money-saving adventure!

Breinigsville, PA USA
14 November 2010
249317BV00001B/199/P